May —

To Laurel Nelson-Rowe,

A woman with a Vision

of her own for the Catholic

Herald! Fr. Guy Gurath

Vern's Vision

An acclaimed weekly news photographer's images of life in small-town Wisconsin

Photographs by Vern Arendt
Verse by Father Guy Gurath

HIGHER
WORLD
Milwaukee, Wisconsin

Published by
Higher World Publications
1000 W. LaSalle Ave.
Milwaukee, WI 53209

ISBN 0-9701850-0-6 (paperback:alk.paper)
Library of Congress Card
Number: 00-105423

Printed by:
Port Publications, Inc.
125 E. Main St.
Port Washington, WI 53074

Distributed by:
Seaworthy Publications, Inc.
215 S. Park St., Suite #1
Port Washington, WI 53074
(262)-268-9250 PHONE (262)-268-9208 FAX
E-mail: publisher@seaworthy.com
Web: www.seaworthy.com

Dedication

To those who love their ice cream colder,
And see the world with vision bolder!
Behold the lens, the photo "taste,"
Next to text — with little waste.
To those who behold the picture's *soul*,
Their pleasure is the writer's goal.
So raise a toast to all good books,
The best deserve our second looks.
Then, Lord, "All Glory be to Thee!"
The Jesuit motto that sets us free.
As each of us adds, quite reverently:
"Whatever's left, just give to me!"

Introduction

I recall vividly the inaugural speech of President John F. Kennedy outside the White House on that brisk winter day of January 20, 1961. The 43-year-old president was followed to the podium by an 86-year-old American poet who had won the Pulitzer Prize an amazing four times. Robert Frost read his poem, "The Gift Outright" (only sixteen lines long, composed for that historic occasion), and his wondrous words echoed throughout the land:

> *Something we were withholding made us weak*
> *Until we found out that it was ourselves*
> *We were withholding from our land of living,*
> *And forthwith found salvation in surrender.*

Some years earlier, Frost had written his own motto in verses with the unusual title of "Two Tramps In Mud Time." The poem ends with these lines:

> *But yield who will to their separation,*
> *My object in living is to unite*
> *My avocation and my vocation*
> *As my two eyes make one in sight.*
> *Only where love and need are one,*
> *And the work is play for mortal stakes,*
> *Is the deed ever really done*
> *For Heaven and the future's sakes.*

In the '70s the psychologist/sociologist Joseph Campbell would call this *union* of avocation and vocation "following your bliss." Indeed, happy and blest are those who are able to do this.

For over 50 years Wisconsin's most honored photojournalist (working for Wisconsin's most honored weekly newspaper) *has* been able to do this. Vern Arendt, proud World War II veteran, has taken countless photos for the *Ozaukee Press* in a career that started in 1948. As this book goes to press, he's still on the job "where love and need are one, and the work is play…" Vern adds: "I loved making pictures as a kid, and I still love it – because I've always remained a kid at heart!" He has also incorporated into his own life another Robert Frost dictum: "I never dared be radical when young, for fear it would make me conservative when old."

This pure love for photography in itself (a picture *as is*, neither radical nor conservative) is what makes Vern's work so appealing. His photos have that unmistakable "human touch" and reveal Emily Dickinson's insight:

A precious---mouldering pleasure---'tis---
To meet an Antique Book---
In just the Dress his Century wore---
And tell you all your Dreams---were true---
He lived---where Dreams were born---
His presence is Enchantment---
You beg him not to go---
Old Volumes shake their Vellum Heads
And tantalize---just so---

This *partial* tribute to Vern's work (we hope it's simply Volume One) is a glimpse of life captured on film in small-town America over the past 50 years, "In just the Dress his Century wore." The photos were chosen for their *universal* appeal (at least that's our hope), and the pictures are all "in glorious black and white!" As devout movie fans of the golden oldies, we too feel that classics like "Casablanca," "Citizen Kane" and "On the Waterfront" should not be "violated by colorization."

Finally, I was among the privileged 700 to hear America's new poet laureate, Robert Pinsky, read his own poetry at the downtown Milwaukee Public Library on a truly memorable Sunday afternoon, February 20, 2000. His marvelous verses are not only witty and winsome, but also prophetic and profound. My attempts are not in his league, but I do hope their lightheartedness will complement (and compliment) Vern Arendt's wonderful photos, "For Heaven and the future's sakes."

As a closing tribute to "Vern's Vision," allow me to borrow from "Americans' Favorite Poems," edited by Robert Pinsky and Maggie Dietz (director of the Favorite Poem Project, Boston University), and published in 2000. Among those favorites is "Song of the Open Road" by Walt Whitman:

The earth, that is sufficient,
I do not want the constellations any nearer,
I know they are very well where they are,
I know they suffice for those who belong to them.

(Still here I carry my old delicious burdens,
I carry them, men and women, I carry them with me wherever I go.
I swear it is impossible for me to get rid of them,
I am fill'd with them, and I will fill them in return.)

Father Guy Gurath

Camera Controlled

"Ah, at last I think I have my shot!"
Could it, in process, turn to pot?!
"But this is really what I need."
Is that so? Maybe it's just bird-seed!
So what's the difference in this "reality?"
No matter what the artist's mentality.
Is it real? Or merely "realized?"
Is it true? Or simply "lionized?"
Is it a sting? Or just a bee?
Something you experience? Or something you see?
A bee is filmed — a sting is felt!
The first is honey — the second a welt!
So what's the point in all this, if you please?
Are we looking for steak? Or just some cheese?
I answer firmly: "Both are needed in our lives,
Whether we're celibate — or have lots of wives!"
And the bird on soft shirt, clinging quite tight,
Offers sound advice: "Just shoot in black and white!"
Does that mean color is really so bad?
"No, but drama craves its shadows — that's the ad!
You see, it's color that often distracts us.
But here's the essence — simple, clean, no fuss!"

Foreword

Vern Arendt is a news photographer. For more than 50 years, he has had the toughest news photographer's job in the world. I know. I've been his editor for a good many of those years.

Vern hasn't had to patrol the mean streets of a metropolis with his camera, hasn't had to cover violent demonstrations, hasn't had to photograph combat operations (though as an infantryman he fought with distinction in the bloodiest battles of the Philippines in World War II), and that is precisely why his job has been so difficult. A man who prefers action, he would have welcomed assignments in which the news was literally exploding around him. But Vern's beat has always been Ozaukee County, Wisconsin, where the news develops out of the slow rhythms of small-town life. Imagine the challenge of making dramatic, evocative, emotion-filled, prize-winning photographs of a county fair, a high school graduation, a Boy Scout merit badge ceremony or a ground-breaking for a library addition. It is Vern's genius, and his legacy to photojournalism, that he has been able to do that very thing week after week, year after year.

Vern became the one-person photo staff of Ozaukee Press, a weekly newspaper published in the Lake Michigan port city of Port Washington, in the late 1940s. A strapping farm boy from rural Ozaukee County who went to war and came home with a dream of a career as a photographer, he enrolled in Milwaukee's respected Layton School of Art, and graduated with not only the requisite technical skills of photography but a fascination with the creative possibilities of his medium.

Ozaukee Press and Vern Arendt were made for each other. The Press was a radical upstart, the first newspaper in the country to use the photo-offset printing method. The founder, my father, pioneered this newspaper printing method for the express purpose of achieving high quality reproduction of photographs. And Vern, from the day he walked into the newspaper office and asked for a job, has produced photos worthy of the very best reproduction.

No homecoming celebration, no first communion, no prom, no barn-raising, no high school football game, no check presentation, no benefit dance happens in the Press' circulation area without Vern and his camera in attendance. It has not been unusual for a single issue of the Press to contain more than 50 photographs, all bearing the credit line, "Photo by Vern Arendt." Vern's magic is to produce extraordinary photographs of ordinary events.

Shocking, life-and-death news, of course, comes to small towns too, and when it has, Vern Arendt has always been there, recording tragedy, high drama, pathos and heroism with all of the power manifest in black and white photography—and with skill that has won for him a plethora of awards for excellence in spot news photography.

I started this foreword by writing that Vern Arendt is a news photographer, and that he certainly is, but that title doesn't say enough about his work, for he is also a nature photographer whose remarkable pictures of animals and plants, landscapes and seascapes could fill a book of their own. Prowling the back roads of his beloved Ozaukee County farm country, waiting hours in a blind, tramping the marshes, surveying a majestic inland sea from Lake Michigan bluffs, Vern has produced a photographic chronicle of animal and plant "news" events to rival that of the human events he covers.

You will find some of those in this collection, among the many others that capture moments in the lives of people Vern has encountered on his weekly news photographer's beat. These photographs represent but a tiny fraction of the life's work of Vern Arendt, but they are a rich sample nonetheless of an extraordinary photographer's art and the stories it tells of life in small-town Wisconsin. They are presented here with the insightful, often whimsical verse of Vern's good friend, Father Guy Gurath, who was largely responsible for making this book happen.

Bill Schanen
Editor and Publisher
Ozaukee Press

Vern's Vision

Yes, that's Vern Arendt at age four.
Even then he was looking for more!
So, indeed, what's he gazing at?
An upside down, sleeping bat?
His vision so eagerly "on the prize!"
Something not meant for his roving eyes?
So please do tell us: What's so engrossing?
While at home, his Mom is toasting.
Vern should be there now, eating his first meal.
Instead, he's "spying" on something seemingly real.
Well if the truth, as always, must prevail,
It's a vision that makes his young heart sail!
Marilyn's calendar! — Vern's great joy:
"She's really beautiful! Boy, oh boy!"
("Vern's Vision" is a case of poetic license at its best,
For his birthday really makes him a fan of Mae West!
But since Marilyn is more an icon than Mae will *ever* be,
Vern has agreed to *change* his age — so gracefully!)

Perspective

This insight, by Oscar Wilde,
Is for the strong, and the mild:
"Two men looked out of prison bars:
One saw mud, and the other? Stars!"
Some workers see the paycheck alone,
A matter merely of flesh and bone.
A silly surrender to schedule and clock:
"Another day of duty on the dreary dock!"
But others see much more than this,
Capturing even a hint of bliss.
Some endure until retirement yawns,
Others create until Eternity dawns!

Winterized

I saw a sign in mid-December,
The kind a kid likes to remember:
"In Wisconsin's winter, no wimps allowed.
It's only for the hardy — and the unbowed!"
That same day I walked through the woods.
It was really cold — I needed two hoods!
So I asked myself: "What's Florida like?
Any sledding there? Ice-fishing? Frozen pike!
Or is it hot and muggy the whole-year through?
With every sport played indoors? In sweaty mildew!
Well, I think I'll stay and take the cold,
At least for now — but not when I'm old!"

Face Fresh

What a gracious, delightful smile.
For that response, you'd walk a mile!
"Those happy smilets that played on her lip,"
Said Shakespeare, knowing us from toes to tip!
In time do we lose what is best in us?
Leaving our childhood with just a crust!
Or do we *choose* to cling to the best?
"I want my *soul* — take the rest!"
Lots of bad breaks and ill-timed fate
Take their toll on our meager plate.
But some still cling to their youthful dreams,
And all their lives say "yes" to moonbeams!

Michelangelo

Was there *ever* an artist more renowned than he?
Massive muscle — titanic talent — busy as a bee!
The surge of God was always in his hungry hands,
Sculpting Moses, David, Jesus, lions and lambs.
One could touch his wondrous work and proclaim:
"Ah, *true* acclaim, much more than flimsy fame!"
Each and *every* artist strives to be
The very best for all the world to *see*:
The honey hand of God at work in human hands,
Noble — vivid — awesome — it *forever* stands!

Turtle Time

"There's more to life than hype and speed,"
Said the laid-back tortoise, "even if you lead!"
People seem to follow more faithfully
Those who take their time...gracefully.
In a world too weary of rush and haste,
So maddening in worry and waste,
God's "lower" creatures teach this lesson:
"Into so many projects, don't go messin'!
Just take your time and slow it down,
Let your computer be the clown!
It's always rushing, gobbling you up.
You be boss — it's only your pup!"

Boat Boisterous

"Hey, Ray, look up — that ship's almost on us!
We'll be crushed like beetles under a bus!"
Ray, aware his engine has lots of gas,
Keeps on fishing: "He's got lots of room to pass!"
The ship with the name of Henry H. Rogers,
Keeps on churning, hoping its victims are dodgers!
Then, in a second, the fishermen speed away,
Tasting the freedom of another fine day!
The "Titanic" too maintains its regular rounds,
So proud of its bow — awesome "blood-hounds!"

Home

The simple look — without pretension.
Like all true things — no condescension.
Every great person, looking back,
Asks directly: "What did I lack?"
Then: "Nothing, really. It was all there,
All the ingredients that made me dare...
Go beyond neighborhood and small town,
Pursuing a dream after cap and gown."
The very meekness of our origins, it seems,
Is the best beginning for impossible dreams.

Dogged By A Cat

"I'm your classic curious cat.
What do you think of that?"
Docile dog: "Buzz off, smart ass.
Your breath's as bad as your gas!"
Is this too harsh for the friendly dog?
Or is it the cat that lives in a fog?
Must the mild-in-manner take it all?
Or is it better to show some gall?
How *do* "the meek inherit the earth"?
By mocking the mighty — and keeping the mirth!

Future Fired

What's more frightening than a fast fire?
Burning everything — a funeral pyre!
One moment, all seems calm and well.
The next? A clanging fire bell!
The explosion of a faithful, humble barn,
And expletives much harsher than "oh, darn!"
Can everything change this quickly?
When all our dreams turn pale and sickly.
Ah, yes, we know too well this tragic scene,
As lives *plummet* to the lowly and lean.
So...what do we do at a time like this?
Pray for courage to conquer "Satan's hiss!"
What is that? You ask, surmising it's despair,
The opposite of *hope*, the rope to everywhere!

Outhouse On Ice

On impulse, a farm boy pushed it in,
More than temptation, it was a sin!
A tired father came home that night,
His angry cursing was at its height:
"Was it you, boy? You know what I mean."
The lad looked down as truth turned lean.
Then: "Yeah, it was me, Pa. I cannot lie.
Like George Washington, I'm a good guy!"
The father's belt flew off, ready for action,
As the boy cried out in less than a fraction:
"But Washington's pa never hit him — why beat me?"
"Right, son, but neither was he in that cherry tree!"

Tracks Twisted

This railroad yard seems cold and hard,
In need of verses from the bard:
Yes, dear Shakespeare, we do need thee
To bring spirit and sparkle to land and sea!
Some would say: "Let this yard be.
It's beyond repair — so woefully!"
Others counter: "No, let's reclaim it.
Build a park — and then rename it!"
What do we do with our twisted tracks?
That foul our lives — behind our backs!
King Lear says: "Bad is the trade that plays the fool to sorrow."
What's our other choice? *Rebuild* — today and tomorrow!

Shiner Shared

"Oh, oh, Dusty, now my eye looks like yours.
Why did I chase you? — and hit my open drawers!"
Devoted Dusty, sitting near his "fractured" friend,
Seems to say: "For real speed, I'm the one to send!"
That night the battered boy said his prayers.
While on his knees, there were no airs!
His eye was hurting, looking for rest,
And searching Scripture, he found the best:
"Like a green olive tree in the house of God,
I trust in His mercy *forever*." That's mod!
Actually, it's from the great Psalm fifty-two,
Terrific consolation for those in rue:
"So thank You, gracious Lord, for loving me.
For Dusty too, so *precious* to me — like Thee!"

Danes Disciplined

"And if you guys don't play your guts out,
You won't be here to see the next bout!"
A rousing speech by Vince Lombardi,
To five Great Danes, attentive and hardy!
Everyone in America knows this famous story
Of the New York Italian — and Green Bay's glory!
Indeed, they both are quite a sight to behold:
Disciplined Danes — and Packer Green and Gold!
So, dear Vince, wherever you are,
In Heaven, or regions hot and far!
Remember us here, still battling and battered,
Reading the book, "When Pride Still Mattered."
It's by David Maraniss, Pulitzer Prize winner.
His praises would earn your command to dinner!

Quarterback On Cue

Crusty coach: "What happened?
    That last sack!"
"I wish I knew," replied the baffled
    quarterback.
"Don't try to be Brett Favre or
    Dan Marino,
Or this game is definitely over...*fino!*"
"I'm not trying to be," said the
    tough kid,
"But I would like to get a play-off bid!"
So the dialogue went, to and fro,
It was a high school game, not a pro.
Then, finally: "And take your hands
    outta there!"
"But, coach, they're cold when they're
    so bare."
"Well, bud, your status could be
    beyond repair.
We're on TV tonight...*images* are
    everywhere!"

Girls Galore!

What's more beautiful, all in a row?
Than twenty-four girls at the top of their show!
The band plays on — the players too,
As the chorus line, right on cue,
Sings its chant in lovely limbs:
"It's better than a thousand gyms!"
So let the boys too receive their due,
Their glories indeed are all too few.
But the memories of this lovely line
Will live forever — glorious gold mine!

Romance Remembered

Prom night...many years ago.
Feel the music...feel the flow!
Where are all those "dancin' dreams?"
Covered now with smoke and creams!
Our precious plans all gone awry,
As we look back with tears of "why?"
Do these dreams *ever* let us go?
Are they too high? Or we too low!
Shall we go back to yesteryear?
Or dream today? With hearts more clear!

Dogs Divine

"Dog is God spelled backward!"
A smart dog-lover told his pet bird.
The parrot, like a pitcher going to bat,
Replied: "I wonder if God knows that!"
Indeed, the Lord knows dogs are divine,
Marvelous mixtures, like good wine!
For creation is blest with various dogs,
And they're better-looking than hunky hogs!
So whatever size or shape the dog may take,
Cute and cuddly, or big enough to make your shake!
Please remember: Take good care of them
Each a gift — a dependent gem!

We Two

Genesis says: "Do not be on your own...
Flesh of my flesh — bone of my bone!"
It's not good for humans to go solo,
Like a single pony trying to play polo!
A loving Lord, you surely must see,
Designed us as "we" — and not just me!
That attraction called "chemistry"
Is really a reflection of Divinity!
So let's relax and let it be.
Soon these two will be three!
And the love that creates this "trinity"
Is just a small part of a marvelous mystery!

Sacred Cities

Is any city really sacred? Is Rome?
Mecca? Bethlehem? Jerusalem? Home?
All our cities include both saints and sinners,
But the "losers" seem to outnumber the "winners!"
Every town or village in the whole USA
Deserves a heartfelt "sorry" as well as "hoo-ray!"
And the need for shelter, nourishment and cold beer,
For housing, food and especially good cheer,
Is blessed by the lofty church on the hill:
"It's all yours, my people, but pay the bill!"

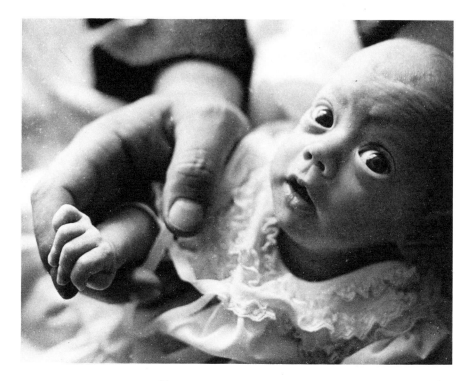

"Honey, Hello!"

What a precious face, so fresh to the world!
Held by her father's hand, in warmth encurled.
Karen Carpenter sang: "We've Only Just Begun,"
As each new infant adds: "This day I too have won!"
Will this "future face" be a parent, painter or teacher?
Whatever he (or she) will be, let's hope it's a "reacher!"
Like a dancer or a diner, out for the night,
Every life must be ready "for the bright!"
So we say to this tiny treasure: "Honey, hello.
We're here to support you, above and below!
And if, in your journey, you hit a snag or two,
We'll still embrace you: Who hasn't missed a cue?!"

Beer Blessed

Ah, at last, the end of a long, tough day.
Takes lots of sweat to bring in that hay!
But now the reward is finally here:
Nothing's better than a barrel of beer!
"Three musketeers," so hearty and hale,
Have a thirst that easily fills a pail!
Every job should have a resounding result.
That's always better than joining a cult!
So: "Three cheers for this barrel of beer,
Which calms all fears — and dries each tear!
And we'll honor *rightly* this barley and hop
By *not* imbibing too much — like a sop!
So thank You, dear Lord, for this beer:
It does renew us with great cheer!"

Mouths Many

"Hey, Mom, I'm really hungry! At least a seed?"
"Easy, baby, there're *lots* of mouths to feed!"
Why such abundance in Creation?
As *millions* struggle for maturation!
Did God make a mistake in calculation?
Or is it *humans* who need liberation?
In Genesis, God says: "Increase and multiply."
But we ask: "Wouldn't it be better to *simplify*?!"
"Of course," says the Lord, "that's exactly the point,
But folks like you are often out of joint!"
"What do You mean?" we ask in a hurried huff,
As we reach for a drink — and another puff!
"Simplify your *own* life, Dear sons and daughters,
And there'll be plenty left over for my 'squatters'!"

Pose Precious

Ah, such simplicity and charm.
All is real — no false alarm!
Now study the poses of most adults.
All that effort — such small results!
Their childhood lost in noise and maze,
Looking like robots in a similar daze!
Why do we lose what is best in us?
Caught by phoniness, such foolish fuss!
But the children laugh in sun and fun.
But we adults? Fools — always on the run!

Ball Battered

"This thing hit me right between the eyes!
As my partner focused on the skies!"
A great game for both amateur and pro,
Golf has few "yes's" but *lots* of "oh, no!"
So why do people play this frustrating game?
Why not try chess? — and feel the same!
But chess lacks the lure of lush-green grass,
Where golfers regularly land on their ass!
So whether playing Pebble Beach or Whistling Straits
(And these world-class courses get lots of eights!),
Golfers everywhere know the feeling of a neat shot:
"After being a *duffer*, it's great to be hot!"

Barn Born!

Can a barn indeed go up this quickly?
Yes, it can — with a group this "thickly!"
Count them and *see* — they're twelve in all.
And that guy on top had better not fall!
Twelve, you see, is a Biblical number,
And no one on this job is ready to slumber!
They're helping their neighbor — without a fee.
Without this help, he'd be "up a tree!"
Harrison Ford was the star in the movie, "Witness."
(He went to Ripon College, for intellectual fitness!)
In the movie's marvelous scene of the barn being raised,
The hero pitches in, working like he's crazed!
The barn went up in quick and noble fashion,
As the workers knew: "We did it with passion!"

Rosary

Beautiful beads, whispered to Mary,
Marvelous mantra, nothing contrary.
Does anyone pray this way anymore?
Or are we too busy? And too poor?
Society sinks lower as everyone scatters,
But Grandmas know: "Prayer really matters!"
"Yes," nods the woman, as old as her beads,
"I still believe — and do my good deeds."
With a faith undaunted over the years,
And a rosary calming all her fears,
She faithfully prays through her tears:
"Bless them all, dear Lord, *all* my dears!
Take care of those still struggling on Earth,
And those too with You, Eternal Mirth!"

Touch Of Tragedy

At first a joke comes to mind:
"A good driver is hard to find!"
But soon all humor fades away,
A tragic lesson is here to stay.
Too many lives are lost like this:
Looking for freedom? A hint of bliss?
The sound of a siren cuts all life...
And laughter — loving — strife.
The empty echo sadly fades away:
"Listen, listen...we're all made of clay!"

Senses Saved

Ah, yes, Helen Keller knew it well,
When Annie Sullivan broke her hell!
Ending isolation and despair,
Interrupting an eternal nightmare!
Miraculous moment! Fabulous feeling!
Blind *eyes* rejoicing in a brand new ceiling!
And Helen "saw" it, *felt* it clearly:
"Taste and touch — hold them dearly!"
Must all our Baptisms be of pain?
Till *we* see our blindness? And disdain!
Or do our "minor" senses teach us?
To honor the "higher" with little fuss!
So let this wondrous body rejoice,
Giving *each* part its proper voice!

Moon Madness

I wonder — is it really true what they say?
"More people begin (and end!) on this day."
The day the full moon begins to appear,
And everything's sharper to eye and ear!
Is this "madness" a hint of Divinity perhaps?
When lovers linger — and runners do extra laps!
Why do we fall in love with the moon?
Ask the dish, who "ran away with the spoon!"
A poet calls the moon God's "pillow talk:"
"It's wonderful outside — let's take a walk!"
And give thanks for this marvelous moon,
Blessing every month with a touch of June!

Foot

A beach should be beautiful, should it not?
No clutter (or clods!), foul fish or rot.
But often the beaches are very bad,
And the feet upon them? Cautious...and sad.
So what's the solution to all of this?
Finding misery when looking for bliss!

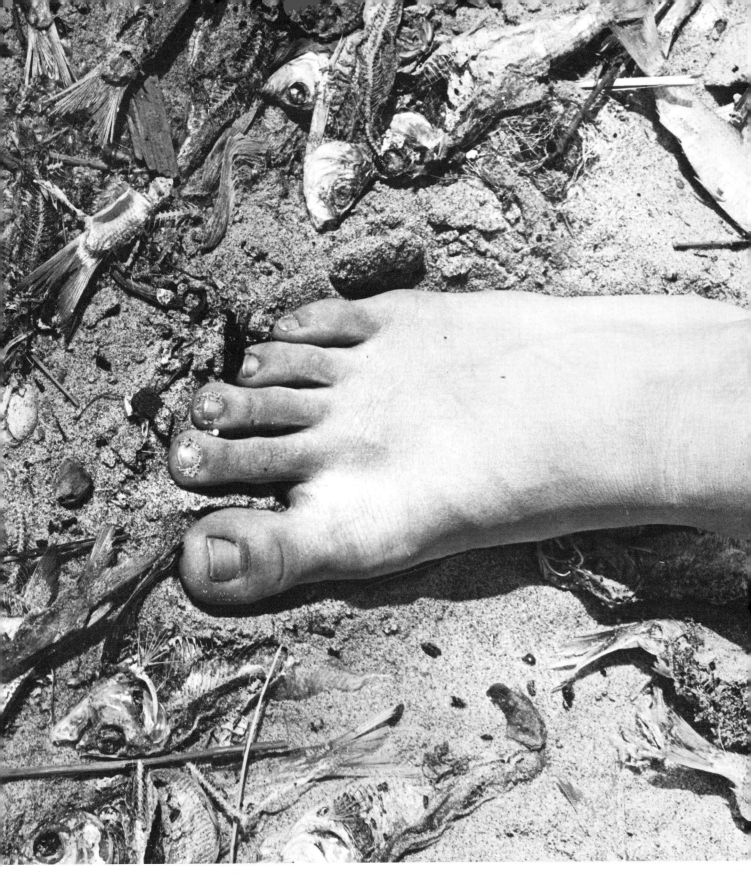

Firm

Is the key to be found in each set of feet?
Deciding to restore — and again make neat!
The foot belongs to a kid with hope:
"There's water here — and I've got soap!
The fish *are* rotten and smell so bad.
But 'clean it up!' I learned from my Dad."

It's Over

Yup, vacation's almost here,
The *best* time of the year!
Books are packed — and teachers too!
No more Mondays: "Why so blue?"
Graduations are often so formal.
They *could* be more fun — and normal!
School too could easily be
Far less rigid — far more free!
"We all learn best," a sage once said,
"When our *heart* guides our head!"

Crystal Contemplation

Ah, what marvelous grandeur and beauty!
Taking us *above* mere schedule and duty.
Saint Francis would know that call,
His love of Nature speaks to us all:
"Preserve, protect, maintain and cherish,
Or God's creation could easily perish!"
Can business and nature have a good marriage?
Fulfilling that song, "like a horse and carriage!"
Are we so dull? And so dense?
So slow to offer our wise two cents!
The choice is really as simple as this:
Surrender to greed — or beauty and bliss!

Where's Mom?

A five-day-old, sandhill crane chick,
New to this world, by nature's pick,
Lost its mother to road-kill,
By a speeding car, too fast for the hill.
And a famous line by Tennessee Williams
(In a poignant play, seen by millions)
Comes to mind in this orphan's dangers:
"I've always counted on the kindness of strangers."
So a weary world is called on once more
To reach out, to rescue and restore
The broken, the abandoned and the lost:
The test of true love — no cost!

Pitch Perfect

"I'm heaving this thing from my toes!
Even my *gut* says 'yes' to my throws!"
Then, waiting for that all-important call,
He hears: "Strike three! That's all!"
Toes and gut then celebrate together,
Hanging in there through all kinds of weather.
The rookie pitcher, with delightful dreams,
Walks from the mound, as light as moonbeams.
He thinks of his hero from bygone days,
Hall-of-famer Nolan Ryan, in lots of displays.
He remembers Warren Spahn and Johnny Sain,
When all the batters chanted: "Pray for rain!"
So, young man, all your lofty ambitions *do* pursue.
As Yogi Berra would say: "Keep pitching — deja vu!"

Eyes Prized

"How do you like this recent creation?
That's a big word for my tiny station!"
The little girl with those big, bright eyes
(Like gazing at the world with two apple pies!)
Knows there's still *lots* to see on planet earth
(The sorrow comes later — *now's* the mirth!).
She looks at everyone with contemplation,
Not yet learning the "art" of reservation.
So, indeed, who has the wiser eyes?
This budding artist? Or her enterprise?
And is she *really* the creator of this art?
Doesn't matter — it's a brand new start!

Goose Gospel

How beautiful this sight of human and goose,
Not one bit uptight, but delightfully loose!
Ah, there's a wonderful lesson here,
In a world overwhelmed by too much beer!
We all know it's the simple things of life
That soften our days of tension and strife.
But we crowd our lives and rush our roads,
And don't even take time to listen to toads!
So the gracious goose does give us reply:
"Take some *time* as everyone rushes by,
Or you'll regret no pause for a friendly 'hi!'
Or even the sharing of some pumpkin pie!
And then you humans, very wise like us geese,
Won't request more protection — or lots of police!"

Chair Chased

"Hey, will you take a look at that?
Some joker got bounced in a spat!"
The passing car was full of four men,
As the quipster added something then:
"Maybe it was yesterday's Packer game,
Where the armchair quarterback came up lame!"
His buddy nudged him, offering a dime:
"Here's your tip — for forcing a rhyme!"
The other two, so somber in the back seat,
Gazed in silence at terrain quite neat.
Yes, it was fall, and all the crops were in,
Far from crowded cities, with noise and din.
It was good to stop and contemplate,
Even if the other two did not commiserate!

Doberman Dour

Ah, the sharp, straight eyes of a Doberman.
When you meet him, better be a sober-man!
How does the world appear to a dog's keen eyes?
Surveying the landscape — "eyes on the prize!"
Yes, the dog is both a pet and predator,
A household habit and useful "editor,"
Teaching us to cut out the flimsy things,
And focus on sounds with the truest rings.
That's the vibrant value of dogs and cats:
Keeping us (and our kids) more human — not brats!
And even this Doberman, with piercing eyes,
Can teach us the value of quick good-byes!

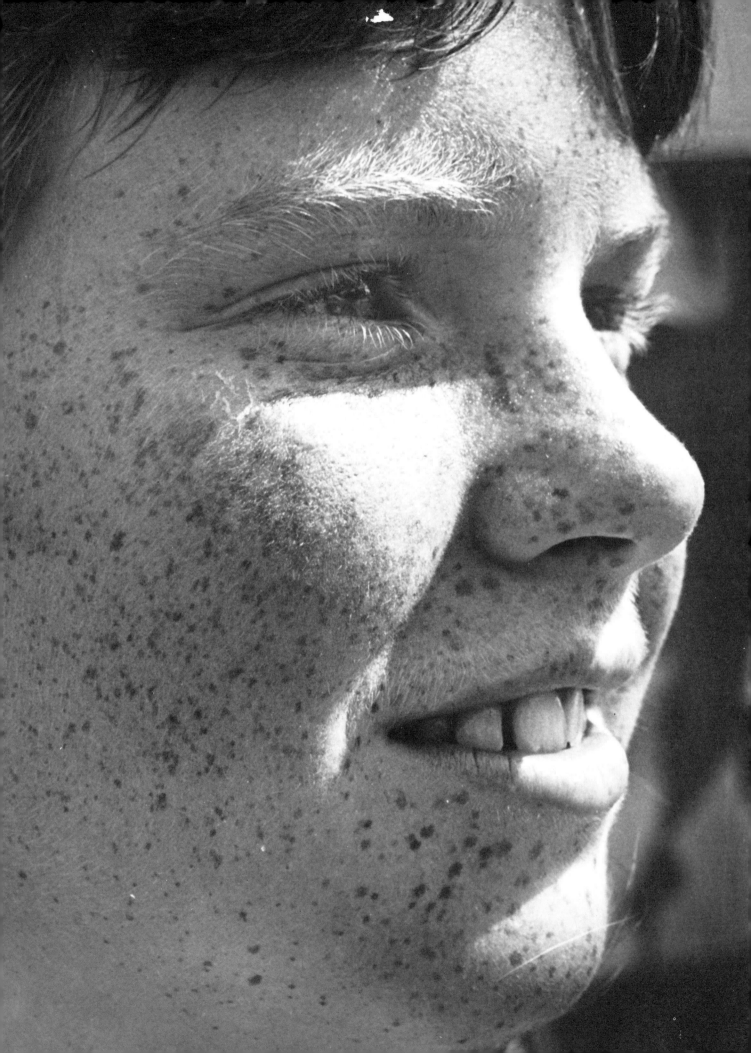

Vision Vibrant

First impressions, far from grace:
Viewing this photo — "Freckle face!"
What a tiny part of the total picture:
Yeast in dough is not the whole mixture!
Just as "attitude is everything,"
And a tuned ear hears each ring,
So wisdom seeks a *worldwide* vision,
Refusing to accept disruptive division.
Freckles too have their own neat charm,
And to *genuine* folks sound no alarm.
So let feeble fools distort the focus,
Drowning in their own hocus-pocus!

Owl Outlook

Two observant owls, from the same brood,
Peering at the world, in a somber mood.
What feature about them, so high in a tree,
Makes them so enchanting to you and me?
They seem, from below, both wise and reserved,
And no telling their age — they're well-preserved!
But don't get too close, or you'll hear a speech.
It'll chill your bones, like a well-oiled screech!
So what's the lesson in all this? you ask,
As the owls converse about their task:
"Simply study us — and *learn* from our reserve.
But don't go meddling — and get what you deserve!"

Heroes Humane

The anxious cop: "Poor guy, let's get him *outta* there!"
A freakish accident has him trapped in a truck's "lair."
"Easy does it, men — I think it's properly angled,"
Then, to himself: "I hope he's not too badly mangled!"
Called the "arrows of outrageous fortune," so rightly,
The nightly news portrays them far "too brightly!"
The quiet agonies of those on the sickly scene
Never translate very well to the TV screen.
But here the story ends on a high and happy note,
The man recovers with a smile — "I'm ready to vote!"
So a triple "Bravo!" to these sturdy and stable men,
Who rescue these victims from the "lion's den!"

Ageless Aging

After fifty years he's still pitching,
Without his muscles even twitching!
"Hell," he says, his arm more solid than weighty,
"If God is willing, I'll be pitching at eighty!"
From the mound, he's still *enjoying* his fling,
And aching muscles do heal — even in a sling!
Yes, there are those who mellow with age,
And follow the lead of Satchel Paige!
They feel their best when in their sync,
Knowing that youth and age have this link:
Time and talent must work together,
As all of life *flies* on a feather!

Window Weary

Your first impression of this photo?
Is it artistic? Or done by Quasimodo!
A haunting image captured by our dreams?
Where reality is always *more* than it seems!
Doesn't every picture strive for this?
The core of bleakness — then of bliss!
To see with *soul* — ah, that's the point.
Otherwise the camera is out of joint!
The world is too full of junk and bluster,
But still cries out for beauty and luster!
So, dear artists, *not* blest with fleeting fame,
Do keep striving — the key to lasting acclaim!

Midnight Mass

Doesn't every memory need a "tent"?
To enclose our dreams with tender scent.
Like Christmas carols night and day,
With Bing Crosby's "Going My Way"!
Rushing shoppers, now turned soft,
Fill the churches, even the loft!
And the preachers, Godly-sent,
Pray for sinners, Heaven-bent!
While nations everywhere this night
Honor infant Jesus, God's delight!

Fisherman Female

Did St. Peter make a living like this?
Waiting for Jesus — and hints of bliss!
I sometimes wonder—know what I mean?
As I see these men, so tough and lean.
Do they ever think of their women back home?
Who clean their catch — but long to roam!
Or do these men, so coarse and callow,
Think of all us women as so much fallow?
Well for me, while pondering my maturity,
I foresee a female fisherman — whoopee!
Then the men in the other boats will help me,
And *together* we'll fish a brand new sea!

Care Cures

"Easy, sweetheart, this is going to help you,"
Says a wildlife rehabilitator, her voice a woo.
An injured, red-tailed hawk is gently fed,
Its weary wings for now are "put to bed."
Lovers of Creation, in every corner of the earth,
Work together to *restore* lost freedom and mirth!
What is better in this worn and worried world
Than bringing new life to the cold and curled?
The Plan Divine, so evident in glorious Eden,
Was spoiled as God inquired: "Was this garden peed in?!"
We call it Original Sin, begun in human pride,
Arrogance really: "All the power's on *our* side!"
But humble humans like St. Francis and (here) Jean Lord
Form "Nature's Committee," Saviors of the Board!

Pizza Pizzazz!!

Pride of performance glows from his face,
His patrons proclaiming: "Food grace!"
Martin Luther King once said (I'm commentating,
Trying to "add" to his marvelous narrating):
"If a man is called to be a street-sweeper"
(An honest job is better than a wimpy weeper!),
"He should sweep the streets as Michelangelo painted."
(When this happens, his supervisors will have fainted!).
"He should sweep the streets so well"
(That's far better than saying "go to hell!"),
"That all the hosts of heaven and earth
Will pause to say" (amid much joy and mirth):
"Here lived a great, devoted street-sweeper!"
Indeed, a worker whose *attitude* went deeper!

Photo Future

Our photo man, next to Miss Wisconsin,
Many years ago, when a Ford had a fin!
They smile together at the great world tide,
And later on go for a very long ride!
The years have passed, some added wrinkles too,
And she and he have weathered a storm or two.
Both have gone their separate ways,
But never forgot those bygone days.
"The past, the present and future — all three shall strive in me!"
Charles Dickens said that in "Christmas Carol" — insightfully!
So carry on, both young and old,
And deepen your faith in a future bold!

Hawk Hooray!

"Easy, Henry Hawk, that's my arm you're holding.
Better not grip any tighter — you'll get a scolding!"
He's smiling, of course — he knows these birds:
"They' both have real class, not like other turds!"
And why does he call this bird Henry Hawk?
"Like Henry Aaron, he performs without a squawk!"
The other one he calls, so rightly: "Sam the squeaker.
Always squawking — he'd never understand 'meeker!'"
They're birds of divergent characters and voices,
Just like humans, who make such similar choices.
Any message for us, Henry Hawk and Sam the Sad?
They reply in unison: "Enjoy us, but don't make us mad!"

Teacher's Time

Ah, that lovely look of admiration,
Soon lost on the way to "maturation!"
That spark, that beauty, gaze and joy,
All is genuine — nothing a ploy!
What happens on the way to maturity?
When youth is captured by stupidity!
Why do hearts turn dark and dense?
Crushing joy and all good sense!
Is TV to blame? Our cluttered culture?
Let's get them back — and beat the vulture!

Bus Blues

More memorable photos are caught by luck and accident
Than are ever planned on purpose and sheer intent!
The lower-lad on the left seems free and easy,
While his buddies on board are just as "breezy!"
The end of the school day is always much better
Than the beginning, when everyone's deader!
And what shall we say about the distracted driver?
Who struggles for sanity everyday — a real "striver!"
The "funny face" on the right is truly symbolic,
Capturing all his friends' feelings, hyper-bolic!
So let teachers relax and enjoy these silly exaggerations,
As they wait for genuine miracles — children's maturations!

In Tune

Ah — what a marvelous face!
Any bitterness? Not a trace!
Totally in tune with her violin.
Not to play it would be a sin!
This must be the key to sanity,
And the remedy for foolish vanity:
Losing ourselves in a higher bliss,
Restoring all that has gone amiss!
"Clean for the Sake of the Dream!"
Actually *being* what we seem!

Sassy Supreme

This "honey horse" has the odd name of "Sassy."
A *better* name would be a lot more classy!
Just look at that intelligent, fabulous face,
As if God had said: "Any defect? Not a trace!"
"Hippotherapy" is the program served by Sassy,
Making this horse much prouder than Lassie!
It gives some injured kids a chance to be free,
As their face and voice erupt in "whoopee!"
They ride so high on mellow mares and gentle geldings,
That horse and rider turn into marvelous "meldings!"
What is better than seeing the world up high in a saddle?
From *that* perspective, everything lower is so much prattle!
So, sweet Sassy, "Elegant Equus," *un*like your nebulous name,
You carry riders who truly *love* you — feeling on top the same!

Kids' Kudos

It's June, when schools are closed and doors are open,
And free time is more than trinket and token!
Three inquisitive faces welcome the summer:
"We do like school, but it can be a bummer!"
The battered barn has been around awhile,
Housing tons of hay — and manure, quite a pile!
But kids don't seem to mind, as their faces tell:
"The smell's not so bad — it's better than a school bell!"
So let vacation thrive, and children with smiles,
As their buses get a break from too many miles!
So much of life, we know, is hurried and rushed,
As kids remind us: "Take some time — and don't get crushed!"

Trap Trumped

"It's better to light one candle than to curse the darkness."
That's an ancient Chinese proverb — better than starkness!
It's also the often-quoted Christopher motto,
And a lot more healthy than winning the lotto!
President Ronald Reagan tells his favorite story,
Growing up before his days of White House glory:
"A young boy was sent in spring to clean the barn,
As he greeted all the stinky stalls with 'oh, darn!'
But the 'bravo boy' began to shovel then and there:
'Under all this manure, there's a *pony* somewhere!'"
So too with all the barriers and sand-traps of life,
With their delays, frustrations and lots of strife!
Do we curse our bad luck and ill-timed stroke?
Or do we take our wedge? And give it a poke!
As this photo shows so well, don't you think?
"Better keep on playing — who needs your stink?!"

Scouts Shout!

"Wow — those little cars can really go!
Though my brother said they'd 'never show'!"
To the Boy Scouts of America, a big "hoo-ray!"
They've been around awhile — and still here today!
Capturing lots of attention with a Pinewood Derby,
While preparing salesmen for Hoover and Kirby!
It's true — so very few go on to be Eagles,
But along the way they're kind to Beagles!
So let's all support these good scouts, boy or girl,
Receiving sound direction in a time of swirl!
It's moments in their lives that turn to pearls,
Better than all that time on computers and curls!
But what about their attitude to the gay?
Perhaps they'll change their law — and have the last say!
For don't you see? Both the gay and the straight
Can have the selfsame values — from toes to pate!

Tender Touch

"Hey, Dad, am I doing this right?"
"Yes, son, but not so tight.
Take it easy and squeeze her light,
Or she'll kick you out of sight!"
What happens to our crowded cities?
With little room for goats and kitties!
What happens to our testy urban kids?
With knives and guns beneath their lids!
Shall we bring our farms to towns?
And turn thugs to milkers? Lacking frowns!

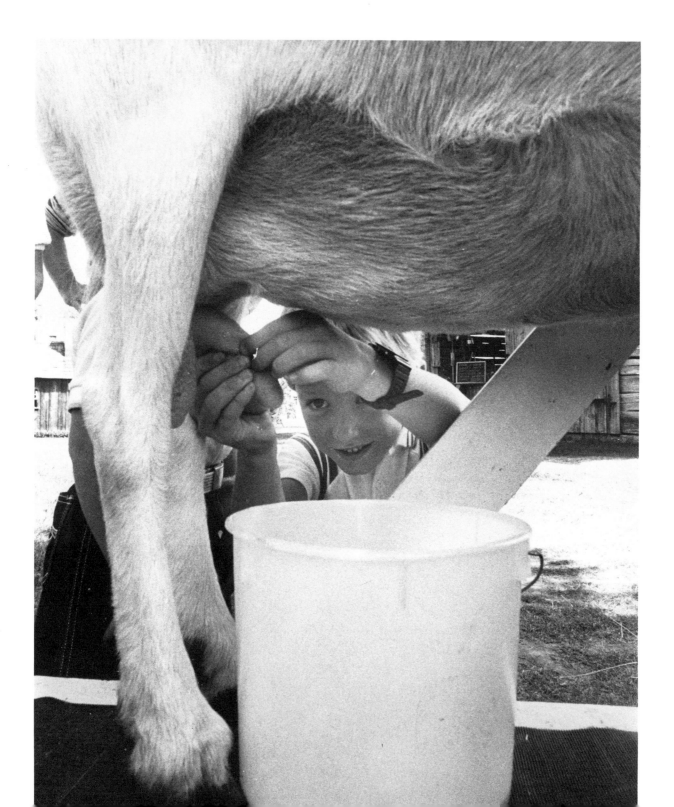

Fulfilled

A bountiful birthday — number ninety-seven!
Everyone together — a hint of Heaven!
And the child in arms, without alarms,
Felt in those hands everlasting charms!
The poet's chant proclaimed a joyful jubilee:
"Grow old with me — the best is yet to be!"
So let the years, with tears and cheers,
Raise a proud salute to wise careers,
That know so well, and proven true:
"We reap what we sow" — and gather our due!

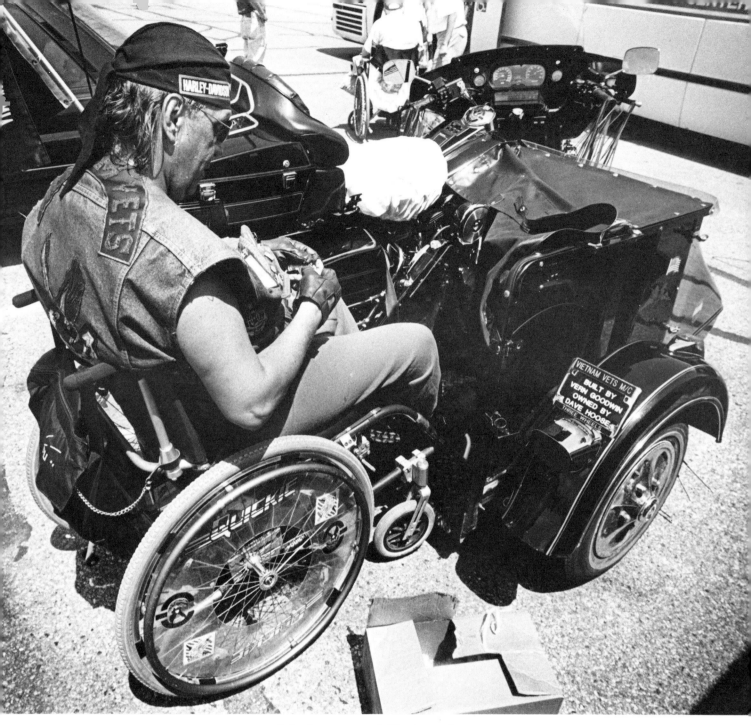

Veteran Victorious

In Vietnam, he landed flat on his back.
Now this Marine's on a different track.
How do we honor those who served America?
First, by putting in place all those in hysteria.
Both those who proclaim: "Our country is everything!"
And those who say: "It doesn't mean a damn thing!"
Isn't there a true and healthy middle ground?
For all those veterans who struggle to be sound?
Doesn't he who has a Harley for legs
Already know that feeling of "living in the dregs"?
"Yeah, man, I gave a hell of a lot over there,
But I'm still here — overcoming despair."
We rightly honor all these gutsy men
By recognizing the price they *still* pay — bodies in a pen.
The Korean War Memorial says it best: "Freedom is not free."
American blood — tons of it! — has been the fabulous fee.

4th of July

Cricket night,
Stars in flight,
Marvelous sight:
"Bombs delight!"
Generations — one.
Conflicts — none.
Peace — won.
Day — done.
Shall we play taps?
Let it go perhaps?
No! Play it for the chaps
Who loved America's maps.
Their blood has filled our gaps!
Yes, honor *them* with tender taps.

Holy Horizon

We who walk and work on the shore
Carry the heartache: "There must be more!"
Why do we weep at times like this?
Our lives "secure" but hearts amiss.
Why do we sigh for times gone by?
Our dreams denied — weak alibi!
Why does the sea, this sacrament,
Call to us? Heaven-sent!
"There's still time," cries the sky.
"Do it now! Before you die!"